Who Said That?

Wisdom passed down by the truth seekers.

By
Michael James McCartney.

For my wife, Yvonne.

Acknowledgements

I would like to thank Rose, (mum), my father's first wife for my upbringing, and my two big Sisters, Pat and Linda, without whose love, patience, and dedication, I feel I may well not be here today.

I love them deeply, as I do my birth mother Joyce, and my father Alf. As you will see in the book, my father started me on my journey of discovery and inquiry when I was in my teens.

Our five children; Sons Dan, and Paul (in spirit, passed 1982), and our daughters Traci, Michele and Lisa. Thank you for your love and constant contributions that enrich and strengthen our family, as well as your individual characters and the knowledge you give to me on a daily basis, and the learning from which I am still experiencing today.

Which leads to our five grandchildren; Madonna, Joshua, Shannon, Rocky, and Phoenix. They are the lights in my life, and I am truly blessed to be able to experience the early years of our children once again, even though they are so individual and a reflection of their parents. I know I speak for my wife Yvonne also in stating, we are both looking forward, and hoping for more grandchildren in the future.

And Yvonne, thank you for just being yourself. I wouldn't change you or anything, for anything! This book is for you and dedicated to you.

I also would like to thank the divine creator, whomever she or he is, with all my being.

Welcome to Who said That? It's a book of quotes that have huge importance on our world, and our understanding of it. I can't tell you how pleased I am that you've found me: suffice to say, I really hope you enjoy this collection made up by the famous, the infamous, the good, the heinous, and many more.

Never underestimate the power of a good, well-placed, and well-timed quote. From scathing wit to powerful motivation, and from social media influencers to world leaders – dropping a meaningful phrase always goes down well.

This collection represents the people and words that have moved (and entertained) me most. Some have challenged me to stop and reflect on the connotation in which they were originally written – and their relevance today. Others have made me laugh out loud. And some have inspired me to do better and be better. I know I will have succeeded if just a few encourage you to do the same.

The wisdom contained in many of these quotes, some of which are hundreds and even thousands of years old, are as relevant and prevalent today as when first written.

I have endeavored to track down and attribute the original source to each quote, but in some cases where this was not possible, I have left them miscellaneous.

Happy days (my personal mantra).

Michael James McCartney.

How it works

Usually with a book of quotations, you'll find orderly groupings and chapters of neatly listed quotes in relevant categories. In Who said That? there is no set course! As you flip to any page, you'll find a random selection to motivate you in ways you were least expecting and to give you food for thought. It's that simple!

The quotes

1. Corinthians 13:1

"Love.

And now I will show you the most excellent way.

If I speak in the tongues of men or of angels, but do not have love, I am only a resounding gong or a clanging cymbal. If I have the gift of prophecy and can fathom all mysteries and all knowledge, and if I have a faith that can move mountains, but do not have love, I am nothing. If I give all I possess to the poor and give over my body to hardship that I may boast, but do not have love, I gain nothing.

Love is patient, love is kind. It does not envy, it does not boast, it is not proud. It does not dishonour others, it is not self-seeking, it is not easily angered, it keeps no record of wrongs. Love does not delight in evil but rejoices with the truth. It always protects, always trusts, always hopes, always perseveres.

Love never fails. But where there are prophecies, they will cease; where there are tongues, they will be stilled; where there is knowledge, it will pass away. For we know in part and we prophesy in part, but when completeness comes, what is in part disappears. When I was a child, I talked like a child, I thought like a child, I reasoned like a child. When I became a man, I put the ways of childhood behind me. For now, we see only a reflection as in a mirror; then we shall see face to face. Now I know in part; then I shall know fully, even as I am fully known.

And now these three remain: faith, hope and love. But the greatest of these is love."

1st Corinthians 13, 1-13, New International Version.

(For me, this is the most profound piece of writing I have ever read – author).

2. "My conscience will simply not allow me to look the other way."

Dane Wiginton, Researcher and founder of GeoengineeringWatch.org

3. "Memories are the golden thread that connect the living with the dead"

4. "There is a great loneliness in pursuing truth."

Professor Douglas Belmore, Political Activist

5. WWG1WGA
"Where We Go One, We Go All."

Engraved on to a ships bell which belonged to John F. Kennedy (1917-1963), President of the United States of America, 1961-1963).

6. "Like it or not everything is changing. The result will be the most wonderful experience in the history of man, or the most horrible enslavement you can imagine. Be active or abdicate the future is in your hands."

William Milton Cooper (1943-2001), American author and folk hero.

7. "Fluoride seems to fit in with lead, mercury and other poisons that cause chemical brain damage…The effects of each toxicant may seem small, but the combined damage on a population scale can be serious, especially because the brain power of the next generation is critical to us all."

Phillipe Grandjean, Professor of Environmental Health Harvard University.

8. "When I tell the truth it is not for the sake of convincing those who do not know it, but for the sake of defending those that do."

William Blake, (1757-1827), Poet.

9. "Ignorance is a choice."

Thomas Williams, 'Truth, Honour, and Integrity' show investigator/visionary activist.

10. "People hate the truth, luckily the truth doesn't care."

Larry Winget, Professional Speaker.

11. "Tell me about heaven, I'm beginning to forget."

6-year-old boy, leaning over the cot speaking to his baby sister. Geoffrey Cheeseman – friend/mentor.

12. A reporter on the floor of the London stock exchange asks a trader "How much money is actually here?" The trader replied "There's so much money here, you couldn't count it" 1980s.

13. "To say I love you, one must first be able to say 'I'"

Ayn Rand (1905-1982), Writer.

14. "The almighty moves in mysterious ways."

Author's birth mother, Joyce McCartney (1828-1989)

15. "There are two types of people in this world 1) those who do what's right regardless of what they are told and 2) those who do what they are told regardless of what is right. Too many people are type 2, but I hope everyone will become or is type 1."

16. "If most of us remain ignorant of ourselves, it is because self-knowledge is painful, and we prefer the pleasure of illusion."

Aldous Huxley, (1894-1963), American writer.

17. "If you tell the truth, you don't have to remember anything."

Mark Twain, (1835-1910), American Writer.

18. "To remember who you are, you need to forget who they told you to be."

19. "If we lose freedom here, there is no place to escape to. This is the last stand on Earth."

Ronald Reagan, (1911-2004), Actor/President of the United States, 1981-89.

20. "Winners never quit, and quitters never win."

Vince Lombardi, (1913-1970), American Football Coach.

21. "Guilt is the only sin you can't enjoy."

Catholic Church.

22. "Would you like a scotch-egg?" "No thank you nanny, I like the egg, but I don't like the scotch."

Author's 6-year-old grandson, Joshua, to his wife, Yvonne.

23. "To learn who rules over you, simply find out who you are not allowed to criticize."

Voltaire, (1694-1778), French writer.

24. "They know the price of everything and the value of nothing."

Reporter referring to the British Government in the 1970s, taken from a broadsheet, regarding the privatization of the nation's resources.

25. "Never worry about fiddling a pound Son, for every pound you fiddle from them, they would've fiddled 10 pound from you."

Alfred McCartney, (1917-1990) author's father, referring to the state.

26. "Everything is seen, and all is known, all will be revealed, and everything shown."

robinhoodrevival.com (Author's former blog)

27. "Those who don't know, don't know that they don't know."

starshipearththebigpicture2012.com

28. "Through every generation of the human race there has been a constant war, a constant war with fear."

Alexander the Great (356BC-323BC), King of Macedon.

29. "History is written by the victors."

Winston Churchill, (1874 -1965) British politician and Prime Minister, 1940-45/1951-55.

30. "It's not black against white; when I say 'we', it's good against evil."

Tupac Shakur (1971-1996), American rap artist.

31. "The laws in Britain are the best in the world for raising money, but for little else."

Taken from the comments section in a British national newspaper, concerning motoring fines.

32. "It is better to remain silent and be thought a fool, than to speak and remove all doubt."

Abraham Lincoln, (1809-1865), President of the United States 1861-65.

33. "Never interfere with an enemy when he's in the process of destroying himself."

Napoleon Bonaparte, (1769-1821), French revolutionary and Premier

34. "Bankers own the Earth. Take it away from them but leave them the power to create money and control credit, and with the flick of a pen they will buy it back."

Josiah Stamp, (1880-1941), 1st Baron Stamp, Director, Bank of England.

35. "If we are true to ourselves, we cannot be false to anyone."

William Shakespeare, (1554-1616), English poet and playwright.

36. "Remember the game is for elected leaders to take all the blame, while the real powers never run for office and control finance and the media"

37. "Am I doing the right thing?"

Author's note: Imagine how often we've posed that question to ourselves, only to discover that indeed we were.

38. "Humans have been domesticated."

Author's note: Take a look at the world we live in; the abject poverty for so many; the restraints that society has placed on our lives; laws dictated by the wealthy then ratified by politicians, that bankers and corporations own.

39. "Don't ever think that these people are clever."

Alfred McCartney (1917-1990), author's father, referring to people who have gone through the system, programmed by education, taught to pass exams, and finally leaving their reality and reasoning in the waste-paper basket.

40. "The constitution is not a suggestion."

Katrina Pierson, American consultant.

41. "Accuse your opponent of what you are doing, as you are doing it, to create confusion."

S. Alinski, Rules for Radicals.

42. "If you climb in the saddle, be ready for the ride."

John Wayne, (1907 – 1979), American actor.

43. "God never sleeps, he only wears pajamas."

Sandra Wright, nursing sister.

44. "How many people has the Queen taken out of poverty?"

Australian citizen's reply when asked by the British press, his thoughts regarding the monarchy.

45. "In any race, if you own all the runners, then you own the winner."

Alfred McCartney, (1917-1990) author's father.

46. "It wasn't the coronavirus that sent us rushing to the supermarkets, it was the media."

Taken from the comments section of a David Icke video, March 2020.

47. "I will splinter the CIA into a thousand pieces and scatter it into the wind."

John F. Kennedy (1917-1963), President of the United States of America, 1961-1963).

48. "So Jesus said to his disciples, 'Go take the word (love) to the towns and villages, and if the people are not interested, dust the sand from your feet and move on'".

An interpretation and message from Geoffrey Cheeseman, author's friend and mentor.

49. "The illiterate of this century will not be those who cannot read or write they will be those who cannot unlearn the lies."

Thomas Williams, 'Truth, Honour, and Integrity' show investigator/visionary activist.

50. "Increased awareness is the antidote to brainwashing."

51. "Compound interest is the 8th wonder of the world. He who understands it earns it, he who doesn't … pays it."

Albert Einstein, (1879-1955), physicist.

52. "They laugh at me because I'm different and I laugh at them because they're all the same."

Kurt Cobain, (1967-1994), American singer/songwriter.

53. "The first step to resolving any problem is to recognize there is one."

54. "I don't want you to think like me, I just want you to think."

David Icke, journalist/writer/activist.

55. "Thinking has become an anachronism."

Author, May 2020.

56. "If you're not on message, you're not mentioned."

robinhoodrevival.com, Author's former blog, describing how David Bellamy, botanist, and Nigel Lawson, politician, were ostracized by state media for describing global warming as "nonsense" on mainstream television.

57. "No problem can be resolved from the same level of consciousness that created it."

Albert Einstein, (1879-1955), physicist.

58. "The definition of the word 'job': just over the breadline."

59. "Up to 80 percent of channeled messages from spirit are not of the light."

One medium's comprehension of the battle between the forces of light and dark in the early 2000s, and how the dark had infiltrated the light to tell 'light workers' what they wanted to hear, not what they needed to."

60. "When you control the media, you control the narrative. Many folks now rely on the MSM not just for their news, entertainment and information, but for further instruction."

Author, April 2020.

61. "If you don't understand it's over. The release of details on the Flynn case paint a horrific picture of corruption, entrapment and blatant criminality on behalf of the F.B.I. and it will only get worse. This is where the dam breaks and the flood begins."

Tweeted by @FollowThe17, April 27th, 2020.

62. "Between the two evils, I always like to take the one I've never tried before."

Mae West, (1893-1980), American actress.

63. "Men fall in love with their eyes, and women fall in love with their ears."

Ken Weeks, author's friend/mentor.

64. "Education means the training of animals."

Thomas Williams, 'Truth, Honour, and Integrity' show investigator/visionary activist.

65. "Fortunately, some are born with spiritual immune systems, that sooner or later, give rejection to the illusionary worldview grafted upon them from birth through social conditioning. They begin sensing that something is amiss and start looking for answers. Inner knowledge and anomalous outer experience show them a side of reality others are oblivious to, and so begins their journey of awakening. Each step of the journey is made by following the heart instead of the crowd, and by choosing knowledge over the veil of ignorance."

Henri Bergson (1859-1941), French philosopher.

66. "Never argue with stupid people, they will drag you down to their level and then beat you with experience."

Mark Twain (1835-1910), American writer.

67. "My dear, you were not brought into this world to work a 40-hour week for the next 50 years and give half your income to the Rothschilds."

Author, 2019.

68. "Reform can only come about when injustice is exposed."

Julian Assange, editor/activist.

69. "A system cannot fail those it was never built to protect."

70. "When we talk about compassion, we talk in terms of being kind. But compassion is not so much being kind; it's about being creative enough to wake a person up."

Chogyam Trungpa Rinpoche (1939-1987), teacher.

71. "Truth is the new hate speech."

72. "Over and over again, we have seen that, there is in this country, another power than that which has its seat at Westminster. The City of London is a convenient term for a collection of financial interests, which is able to assert itself against the government of the country. Those who control money can pursue a policy at home and abroad contrary to that which is being decided by the people."

Clement Attlee (1883-1967), British Prime Minister.

73. "Our lives begin to end the day we become silent about the things that matter."

Martin Luther King Jr, (1929-1968), American minister/activist.

74. "See, in my line of work, you get to keep repeating things over and over again for the truth to sink in, to kind of catapult the propaganda."

George W. Bush, President of the United States.

75. "Science may have found a cure for most evils; but it has found no remedy for the worst of them all… the apathy of human beings."

Helen Keller (1880-1968), American writer.

76. "When what is true comes, what is false must pass away."

77. "Warriors are not what you think of as warriors. The warrior is not someone who fights, for no-one has the right to take another life. The warrior for us is someone who sacrifices himself for the good of others. His task is to take care of the elderly, the defenseless, those who cannot provide for themselves and above all the children, the future of humanity".

Sitting Bull (1830-1895), Hunkpapa Lakota leader.

78. "Change and the truth are the only constants in the universe."

79. "Remember there is always a price to be paid for remaining silent in the face of injustice; that price is tyranny."

John W. Whitehead, American attorney.

80. "I will expose my father's killers no matter who they are, even if I have to bring down the whole government."

John F. Kennedy Jr (1960-1999), American attorney.

81. "Forty years ago when I started my practice, only 1 in 10,000 children has autism. Today, it's 1 in 1,000. What is the only difference we have seen? The inordinate number of vaccines that are being given to children today. My partner and I have over 35,000 patients who have never been vaccinated. You know how many cases of autism we have seen? Zero. I have made this statement for over forty years: no vaccines, no autism.

Dr. Mayer Eisenstein, (1946-2014), M.D.

82. "I will not wear someone else's fear"

*Poster, illustrating a face wearing a mask,
starshipearththebigpicture.com, May 2020.*

83. "Truth never fears investigation."

84. "Anti-Semitic? It's a trick. We always use it to stifle
legitimate criticism of Jews and Zionist Israel."

Shulamit Aloni, former Israeli cabinet minister.

85. "The future is not something we enter; the future is
something we create."

86."We can accept God becoming man to save man, but not
man becoming God to save himself."

Vernon Linwood Howard (1918-1992), American Teacher.

87. "Donald Trump and General Flynn were so squeaky clean,
they had to create crimes to get them. Barack Obama and Joe
Bidden are so incredibly corrupt, they had to hide crimes to
protect them, and it's all coming out now."

Jim Starkey (@C_3C_3), Tweet, September 23rd, 2020.

88. "Cash is king."

Anonymous, but a favourite of Peter McCartney, author's brother.

89. "One of the first duties of a physician is to educate the
masses not to take medication."

William Osler (1849-1919), Canadian Physician.

90. "As long as it's not hitting old ladies on the head it's okay."

London East End expression, referring to one's criminality.

91. "God will judge our enemies; we will arrange the meetings."

U.S Navy Seal mantra.

92. "Forgiveness is overrated, from the Pope down, we've been anesthetized with this mind-virus that in order to be good people we just put our head down, work hard, die poor and let God do the judging. How convenient for power is that story? A little too convenient. Sold to us by the same people who rape our children and sit on a throne of stolen riches."

93. "Can you spell the last two letters of your postcode? I didn't quite catch what you said." (operator). "S for stupid, D for duck." (Reply of author's daughter, Traci).

94. "Governments tend to adopt the mushroom principle; AKA keep them in the dark and feed them bullshit."

Author

95. "Why vote, it hasn't mattered since 1913."

zerohedge.com96.

96. "Quarantine is when you restrict the movement of sick people; tyranny is when you restrict the movement of healthy people."

The Q Movement, May 2020.

97. "It's the message, not the messenger."

98. "All the new technology is of the past, not the future."

Thomas Williams, 'Truth, Honour, and Integrity' show investigator/visionary activist.

99. "If a free society cannot help the many who are poor, it cannot save the few who are rich."

John F. Kennedy (1917-1963), President of the United States of America, 1961 – 1963).

100. "Truth is weirder than any fiction I've seen."

Hunter S. Thompson (1937-2005), American journalist.

101. ""Never be afraid to try anything new remember amateurs built the ark… professionals built the titanic."

102. "What you believe to be true, is it true? Or, do you just believe that it's true because you were taught that and never looked any further?"

103. "I (God) do not call the qualified, I qualify the called."

"Conversations with God", Neil Donald Walsh.

104. "Truth is like the sun; you can shut it out for a time, but it ain't goin' away."

Elvis Presley (1935-1977), American singer, actor.

105. "In the councils of government, we must guard against the acquisition of unwarranted interests, whether sought or unsought by the military-industrial complex. The potential for the disastrous rise of misplaced power exists and will persist."

Dwight D. Eisenhower (1890-1969), President of the United States.

106. "Gold is money, everything else is credit."

J. P. Morgan (1837-1913), American financier.

107. "When I'm good I'm very good, but when I'm bad I'm better."

Mae West (1893-1980), American actress.

108. "But then Iraq happened after September 2001, and America claimed that Al Qaeda was there, and we all know that was a lie, and we now know that our own Prime Minister (Tony Blair) deceived the country terribly."

Clair Short, former Secretary of State, UK.

109. "Too much of a good thing, can be a bad thing."

110. "Death is not the greatest loss of life. The greatest loss is what dies inside while still alive. Never surrender."

Tupac Shakur (1971-1996), American rap artist.

111. "Is everything a conspiracy? No just the important stuff."

Jeff Wells, athlete.

111. "Ignore your rights and they'll go away."

113. "The first step to getting what you want is having the courage to get rid of what you don't".

114. "All truth passes through three stages: First, it is ridiculed. Second, it is violently opposed. Third, it is accepted as self-evident."

Arthur Schopenhauer (1788-1860), German philosopher.

115. "When you assume the appearance of power, people soon give it to you."

116. "Remember it doesn't take a rocket scientist to understand. The only reason the government would want to disarm you after 234 years is because they intend to do something that you would shoot them for."

Twitter, @63Brass, May 2020

117. "By the time you've thought about it, they've done it."

Author, referring to children and their antics.

118. "If we can accept that we are the sum total of all past thoughts, emotions, words, deeds and actions, and that our present lives and choices are colored or shaded by this memory bank of the past, then we begin to see how a process of correcting or setting aright can change our lives our families and our society."

Morrnah Nalamaku Simeona (1913 – 1992).

119. "We have what we call here citizen journalists, because the journalists we have in our media did a disservice to themselves."

General Michael Thomas Flynn, former National Security Advisor to the Trump White House.

120. "The further a society drifts from the truth, the more it will hate those who speak it."

George Orwell (1903-1950), author.

121. "You only get flak when you're over the target."

122. "We are such stuff as dreams are made on; and our little life is rounded with a sleep."

Prospero in 'Tempest', William Shakespeare (1554-1616) English poet and playwright.

123. "News organizations are political activists."

124. "The moon is too big to be natural. The laws of nature dictate it cannot be a fixed planet showing one side only, it is impossible. It is a fixed satellite station only for facing one way."

Thomas Williams, 'Truth, Honour, and Integrity' show investigator/visionary activist.

125. "The government was set to protect man from criminals and the constitution was written to protect man from government."

Ayn Rand (1905-1982), Writer.

126. "Fear is a liar."

127. "Ask not for whom the bell tolls; it tolls for thee."

128. "If you can remember your past, you can remember your future; it therefore follows that you can remember everyone's past and everyone's future."

Stephen Hawking (1942-2018), physicist.

129. "Condemnation without investigation is the height of ignorance."

130. "A king does not kill messengers."

Alexander the Great (356-323BC), King of Macedon.

131. "If you don't conform, you don't perform."

Author. You have to be on message and conform to the controlled politically correct narrative, perverse in today's society (author's note).

132. "You have enemies? Good. That means you've stood up for something, sometime in your life."

Winston Churchill (1874-1965), British Prime Minister.

133. "Don't vote, it's the only vote we have."

Author.

134. "Remember, doing a lot more doesn't mean you're getting a lot more done."

Denzel Washington, American actor.

135. "If you fail to plan, you are planning to fail."

Benjamin Franklin (1706 -1790), American polymath and founding father.

136. "When a well-packed web of lies has been sold gradually to the masses over generations, the truth will seem utterly preposterous and its speaker a raving lunatic."

Dresden James (1923-2008), British novelist/writer.

137. "Read everything; listen to everybody; believe nothing unless you can prove it with your own research."

William Milton Cooper (1943-2001) American author, American hero.

138. "There are three classes of people; those who see, those who see when they are shown, and those who do not see."

Leonardo da Vinci (1452-1519), Italian renaissance polymath.

139. "Two percent of the people think; three percent of the people think they think, and ninety five percent of the people would rather die than think."

George Bernard Shaw (1856-1950), English playwright.

140. "Censorship is protecting you from reality."

141. "...all liars shall have their part in the lake which burneth with fire and brimstone."

Revelations 21:8, New International Version.

142. "The greatest prison that people live in, is the fear of what other people think."

David Icke, journalist/writer/activist.

143. "Democracies only work when large swaths of the population are apathetic."

Samuel P. Huntington (1927-2008), American political scientist.

144. "Those who do not think employment is systematic slavery are either blind or employed."

Nassim Nicholas Taleb, essayist.

145. "The arrogance of ignorance."

146. "It is quite a three-pipe problem, and I beg that you won't speak to me for fifty minutes."

Sherlock Holmes, 'The Red-Headed League', Sir Arthur Conan Doyle (1859-1930), author.

147. "Tip the TV in the trash."

Robinhoodrevival.com, author's former blog.

148. "There is no difference between communism and socialism except in the means of achieving the ultimate end. Communism proposes to enslave by force. Socialism by vote; It is merely the difference between murder and suicide."

Ayn Rand (1905-1982), writer.

149. "The poor are inherently honest."

150. "It's not a conspiracy theory when you have proof."

Julian Assange, Wikileaks founder.

151. "Big pharma, sustaining the sickness."

starshipearththebigpiture2012.com.

152. "I have come here to chew bubblegum and kick ass, and I'm all out of bubblegum."

They Live, (movie) 1988.

153. "The deep state is called deep for a reason; it goes deep."

Kerry Cassidy, Project Camelot, 30 April 2020, YouTube.

154. "I warn you of him, and there was no prophet but warned his followers of him; but I will tell you something about him which no prophet has told his followers ad-Dajjal (anti-Christ) is one-eyed, whereas Allah (God) is not."

Hadith Bukhari.

155. "I'm not saying I'm allergic to school, I just don't like it."

Molly Robberts, author's five-year old niece.

156. "You see there's no long-term investment in Britain; the City of London will lend you the money on Monday and want it returned with interest on Friday."

Max Keiser, American broadcaster.

157. "When I despair, I remember that all through history, the way of truth and love has always won. There have been tyrants and murderers and for a time, they can seem invincible. But in the end, they always fail, think of it always."

Mahatma Gandhi (1869-1948), Indian writer, teacher, and activist.

158. "The secret to life is honesty and fair dealings; if you can fake that, you've got it made."

Groucho Marx (1890 -1997), American comedian.

159. "When we come for you, we know who you are, and you know who you are."

Author, referring to bankers – who have dominated, enslaved, and murdered mankind with their wars, pestitude, corruption, falsehoods, and pernicious usury.

160. "Always trust a person looking for the truth; never trust someone who's found it."

161. "Some people think football is a matter of life and death. I assure you, it's much more important than that."

Bill Shakely (1913-1981), Manager of Liverpool Football Club.

162. "Family is everything; everything else is just everything else."

163. "Talk low, talk slow, and don't say too much."

John Wayne (1907-1979), American actor.

164. "I don't want the cure to kill the patient."

Tom Fitton, Judicial Watch March 2020, referring to the coronavirus.

165. "There's nowt queer as folk."

166. "Some people know there is something inherently wrong with this country; however, they don't quite know what."

Jack Hargraves, British television presenter.

167. "If not us, who? If not now, when?"

John F. Kennedy (1917-1963), President of the United States.

168. "Often, when you think you are at the end of something, you're at the beginning of something else."

Fred Rogers (1928-2003), American television personality.

169. "You must unlearn what you have been programmed to believe from birth. That software no longer serves you, if you want to live where all things are possible."

Jacqueline E. Purcell.

170. "Do something unusual today! Think."

171. "We can no longer tolerate the police, policing the police. It's like Jack the Ripper investigating the Whitechapel murders."

robinhoodrevival.com, author's former blog.

172. "We are all geniuses up to the age of ten."

Aldous Huxley (1894-1963), American writer.

173. "I'll try anything one, twice if I like it, and three times to make sure."

Mae West (1893-1980), American actress.

174. "I have a divine right to be wrong, just as I do to be right."

Author, May 2020.

175. "The welfare of humanity is always the alibi of tyrants."

zerohedge.com May 12, 2020.

176. "Low interest rates will take your money, but inflation steals your wealth."

Max Keizer, American broadcaster.

177. "I am the penitent man."

Author.

178. "World Zionism today can best be described as the world's largest organized crime syndicate. They appear to be soulless parasites upon the human race. They are empowered by the Zionist city of London – private central bankers who specialize in Babylonian money – majic, and making money from nothing, (debt-based notes presented as money) and pernicious usury. They are generally recognized by numerous Intel insiders to be parasites on the world; war profiteers and mass murderers behind evert major war, as well as the hidden hand behind most drug trafficking, pornography, sex trafficking, slave labor, massive banking mortgage fraud, and other financial frauds and scams. Using their imaginary, debt-based, pretend money, they have bought and now own almost every single US congressman, most Supreme Court judges, and almost every Federal judge."

Preston James, veteranstoday.com

179. "It's a trick, we always use it. When from Europe if someone is criticising Israel, we bring up the holocaust. When in this country, (USA), then they are anti-Semitic".

Shulamit Aloni, former Israeli cabinet minister.

180. "A man, who stands for nothing, will fall for anything."

Malcolm X (1925-1965), American minister/activist.

181. "Service to others is the greatest service to self."

Sacha Stone, writer/activist.

182. "The truth is what they say it is."

183. "A wise man once said, when life throws dirt at you, clean it off."

184. "It's not where you go, it's who you meet along the way."

The Wizard of Oz, Frank. L. Baum.

185. "Don't worry, bout a thing; cause every little thing, is gonna be alright."

Bob Marley (1945-1981), Jamaican singer/songwriter.

186. "Everything will be alright in the end. And if it's not alright, it's not the end."

Anonymous – often attributed to John Lennon and used in the film 'The Best Exotic Marigold Hotel'.

187. "They hide it right out in the open."

The cabal in a 'freewill universe' have to inform humanity of their intensions, it's the divine law.

188. "To be a spiritual warrior, one must have a broken heart. Without a broken heart and the sense of tenderness and vulnerability that is in one's self and all others, your warriorship is untrustworthy."

Chogyam Trungpa Rinpoche (1939-1987), teacher.

189. "The truth when you finally chase it down, is almost far worse than your darkest visions and fears."

Hunter S. Thompson (1937-2005), American writer.

190. "In the end, we will remember not the words of our enemies, but the silence of our friends."

Martin Luther King Jr (1929-1968), American minister/activist.

191. "If a cluttered desk is the sign of a cluttered mind, of what then is an empty desk the sign of?"

Albert Einstein (1879-1955), physicist.

192. "I did not attend his funeral, but I sent a nice letter saying I approved of it."

Mark Twain (1835-1910), American writer.

193. "It wasn't the virus that crashed the economy, it was the people who obeyed."

zerohedge.com 16 May 2020.

194. "Remember it's like it is because you have let it."

robinhoodrevival.com

195. "If you keep burying your head in the sand, eventually you'll hit a landmine."

starshipearththebigpicture2012.com

196. "I spent 33 years and four months in active military service, and during that period I spent most of my time as a high-class muscle man for big business, for wall street and the bankers. I was a racketeer, a gangster for capitalism."

Major-General Smedley Butler (1881-1940), US Army.

197. "The first person to live to 150 has already been born."

Billboard, California, 2015.

198. "Why is free thought ridiculed, challenged and threatened when a person is opposed to the mainstream narrative?"

The Q Movement, 28th March 2020.

199. "Run to the rescue with love, and peace will follow."

River Phoenix (1970-1993), American actor.

200. "Truth is hate – to those who hate the truth."

Bob Enyart, Pastor.

201. "I have two great enemies; the southern army in front of me and the financial institutions in the rear. Of the two, the one in the rear is the greatest enemy."

Abraham Lincoln (1808-1865), President of the United States.

202. "Alerting the people to the truth comes at an enormous cost."

Thomas Williams, 'Truth, Honour, and Integrity' show investigator/visionary activist.

203. "Politics is the art of looking for trouble, finding it everywhere, diagnosing it incorrectly, and applying the wrong remedies."

Grouch Marx (1890-1997), American comedian.

204. "We went from zero to gestapo overnight."

Spiro Skouras, activistpost.com, 12 April 2020.

205. Sports journalist, to golfer Gary Player: "That was a lucky shot out of the bunker there Gary."

Gary Player: "Seems like the more I practice, the luckier I get."

206. "It doesn't matter if you flip burgers, bricks, or houses; just don't sit on your ass all day flipping channels."

Denzel Washington, American actor.

207. "Today's mighty oak is just yesterday's nut that held its ground."

David Icke, investigative journalist, writer, activist.

208. "It matters not who you love, where you love, why you love, who you love, and how you love. It matters only that you love."

John Lennon (1940-1980) singer/songwriter, activist.

209. "How does the average person, who is under constant financial stress (by design), find time to discern fact from fiction?"

The Q Movement, 28 March 2020.

210. "It's all about love and truth, nothing else matters."

211. "You can't separate peace from freedom, because no one can be at peace unless he has his freedom."

Malcolm X (1925-1965), American minister/activist.

212. "Far too many are content to consent."

213. "The populace has been programmed to believe that information labeled conspiracy theory is worthless, merely ideas springing from addled minds. But this question is logical; why is the possibility that the coronavirus was made in a laboratory in the United States and taken to China simply dismissed as conspiracy theory instead of being investigated?"

Channeled message from the other side of life, regarding the situation humanity finds itself in today, and how the mainstream media describe free thought. – "Matthew", federationoflight.ning.com, May 7th, 2020.

214. "A lie is a lie, even if everyone believes it. The truth is the truth, even if no one believes it."

215. "You cannot go back and change the beginning, but you can start where you are and change the ending."

C.S. Lewis (1898-1963), Irish writer.

216. "Everything you've been led to believe, turn on its head."

Sathya Sai Baba (1926-2011), Indian guru.

217. "The greatest lie ever told is that vaccines are safe and effective."

Dr. Leonard Horowitz.

218. "You can avoid reality, but you cannot avid the consequences of avoiding reality."

Ayn Rand (1905-1982), writer.

219. "In the World War (1), a mere handful garnered the profits of the conflict. At least 21,000 new millionaires and billionaires were made in the United States during the World War. That many admitted their huge blood gains in their income tax returns. How many war millionaires falsified their tax returns, nobody knows? How many of these war millionaires shouldered a rifle? How many of them dug a trench? How many of them knew what it meant to go hungry in a rat infested dug out? How many of them spent sleepless, frightened nights ducking shells, shrapnel and machine gun bullets? How many of them parried a bayonet thrust from the enemy? How many of them were wounded or killed in battle? Out of war, nations acquire additional territory; if they are victorious, they just take it. This newly acquired territory promptly is exploited by the few – the selfsame few who wrung the dollar out of blood in the war. The general public shoulders the bill and what is this bill? This bill renders a horrible accounting. Newly placed gravestones, shattered bodies, shattered minds. Broken hearts and homes, economic instability and depression. All its attended miseries. Back breaking taxation for generations and generations."

Major-General Smedley Butler (1881-1940) U.S Army officer.

220. "When things go wrong, don't go with them."

Elvis Presley (1935-1977), American singer/actor.

221. "It does not take many words to tell the truth."

Sitting Bull, Hunkpapa Lakota Native American leader.

222. "Bankers, we're coming for you."

Author, referring to the belief that the people will eventually rise up against the bankers' tyranny and usury.

223. "Big pharma is about wealth, not your health."

224. "Government is not the solution to our problems; government is the problem."

Ronald Reagan (1911-2004), President of the United States.

225. "You've got to walk the walk when you talk the talk. The worlds full of preachers, but very short of practitioners."

Author, 1990s.

226. "Conspiracy theorist was a term coined by President Richard Nixon. He called Woodward and Bernstein conspiracy theorists when he was getting nicked over the Watergate affair; he also said, 'I am not a crook'. It later transpired he was part of a conspiracy and a crook."

Vinny Eastwood, guerillamedia.co.nz

227. If you haven't read the Q drops QMap.pub, get yourself a real education, it's home schooling for adults."

Starshipearththebigpicture.com, 2 May 2020.

228. "Until they become conscious, they will never rebel; and until they have rebelled, they cannot become conscious."

George Orwell (1903-1950), novelist.

229. "In politics, nothing happens by accident. If it happens you can bet, it was planned that way."

Franklin D Roosevelt (1882-1945), President of the United States.

230. "Every tree, every plant – has a spirit. People may say that a plant has no mind. I tell them that a plant is alive and conscious. A plant may not talk, but there is a spirit in it that is consciousness that sees everything. Which is the soul of the plant, its essence, what makes it alive."

Pablo Amarigo (1938-2009), Peruvian artist.

231. "This above all, to thine own self be true."

William Shakespeare (1554-1616), (Polonius, Hamlet, Act I: Scene III), English poet/playwright.

232. "We are the proud parents of a child who has resisted his teacher's attempts to break his spirit and bend him to the will of his corporate masters."

George Carlin (1937-2008), American comedian.

233. "People were created to be loved. Things were created to be used. The reason why the world is in such chaos, is because things are being loved and people are being used."

John Green, American author.

234. "Being honest may not get you a lot of friends, but it will always get you the right ones."

John Lennon (1940-1980), singer/songwriter, activist.

235. "The only way out of the labyrinth of suffering, is to forgive."

236. "The truth is incontrovertible; malice may attack it, ignorance may deride it, but in the end, there it is."

Winston Churchill (1874-1965), British Prime Minister.

237. "They're not in the liability business."

Peter McCartney (1955-2016), Author's brother, referring to insurance companies and their reluctance to pay out legitimate claims.

238. "Once they start asking for money, forget it."

Sathya Sai Baba (1926-2011), Indian guru, referring to charlatans operating within religion.

239. "There are people whose job it is to be sweet, loving, and caring; and it is the job of warriors to look after them."

Laura Knight, Jadczyk historian.

240. "In refusing to defend Assange, mainstream media exposes it's true nature, because it has no intention of creating an informed populace or holding power to account."

241. "Many are called, but few get up."

Oliver Herford (1863-1935), writer.

242. "Son, you are living in the most corrupt country in the world."

Alfred McCartney (1917-1990), Author's father, describing the United Kingdom in the 1980s.

243. "The program of the ruling elite in Orwell's 1984, was a foot stamping on a human face forever! This is naive and optimistic. No species could survive for even a generation under such a program. This is not a program of eternal or even long-range dominance. It is clearly an extermination program."

William S. Burroughs (1914-1997), American writer.

244. "We don't stop playing because we grow old; we grow old because we stop playing."

George Bernard Shaw (1856-1950), playwright.

245. "There are two ways to be fooled. One is to believe what isn't true, and the other is to refuse to believe what is true."

Soren Kierkegaard (1813-1855), Danish philosopher.

246. "Sometimes, folks are just too frightened to be free."

John Darash, National Liberty Alliance.

247. "The opposite of love is not hate; its indifference."

Elie Wiesel (1928-2019), American-Romanian writer.

248. "This was irregular warfare at its finest in politics."

General Michael Thomas Flynn, former National Security Advisor to the Trump White House.

249. "God will not be governed by time, or place, or circumstance."

250. "It's f**ked how people get judged for being real, and how people get loved for being fake.".."

Tupac Skakur (1971-1996), American rap artist.

251. "Wisdom is knowing how little you know."

Socrates, philosopher.

252. "Obedience is the connective tissue of oppression."

253. "But I'll tell you what hermits' realize. If you go off into a far, far forest and get very quiet, you'll come to understand that you're connected to everything."

Alan Watts (1915-1973), writer.

254. "To dare is to lose footing momentarily; not to dare is to lose oneself."

Soren Kierkegaard (1813-1855), Danish philosopher.

255. "Governments worldwide are struggling to contain a new virus that could have a huge impact on billions of lives worldwide. That virus is called truth."

Thomas Williams, 'Truth, Honour, and Integrity' show investigator/visionary activist.

256. "The real hopeless victims of mental illness are to be found among those who appear to be most normal. Many of them are normal because they are so well adjusted to our mode of existence; because their human voice has been silenced so early in their lives, that they do not even struggle, or suffer, or develop symptoms as the neurotic does. They are normal, not in what may be called in the absolute sense of the word; they are normal only in relation to a profoundly abnormal society. Their perfect adjustment to that abnormal society is a measure of their mental sickness. These millions of abnormally normal people, living without fuss in a society to which, if they were fully human beings, they ought not to be adjusted."

Aldous Huxley (1894-1963), American writer.

257. "Say thank you in advance for what is already yours."

258. "The smallest minority on Earth is the individual. Those who deny the individual's rights cannot claim to be defendants of the minorities."

Ayn Rand (1905-1982), writer.

259. "There is no way to happiness, happiness is the way."

260. "It is not a justice system; it is just a system."

Bob Enyart, pastor.

261. "That's the standard technique of privatization, defund, make sure things don't work, people get angry, you hand it over to private capital."

Noam Chomsky, American philosopher/activist.

262. "When we give of our time, we actually give a portion of our life that we will never take back."

Alexander the Great (356-323BC), King of Macedon.

263. "Those who are able to see beyond the shadows and lies of their culture will never be understood, let alone believed by the mases."

Plato.

264. "The world is a dangerous place; not because of people who are evil, but because of people who don't do anything about it."

Albert Einstein (1879-1955), physicist.

265. "Think before you act. When you sell your soul to the devil, you're not allowed to ask for it back."

Madonna, American singer/songwriter.

266. "When I find myself in times of trouble mother marry comes to me, speaking words of wisdom, let it be, let it be."

'Let It Be', The Beatles.

267. "There is only one race – the human race. Hate is a choice. Love is a choice. I choose love."

John Russell, from the comments section of a YouTube video for Ray Stevens' Everything is Beautiful.

268. "And I looked and behold a pale horse and his name that sat on him was death and hell followed with him."

Revelations 6:8, New American Standard Version.

269. "You don't remember what happened; what you remember, becomes what happened."

John Green, American author.

270. "I'm not afraid of dying, I just don't want to be there when it happens."

Spike Milligan, Irish comedian.

271. "People who are having sex with children are not johns and tricks. They are child rapists and paedophiles, so we should call them what they are."

Jade Pinkett Smith, American actress.

272. "Love you more."

Author's granddaughter, Madonna, after being told "I love you," by her grandfather.

273. "If you don't read the newspapers you're uninformed; if you read the newspapers you're misinformed."

Mark Twain, 1835 – 1910 American Writer.

274. "Ignorance is the single greatest tool of oppression; and…the greatest despondency is the greatest ignorance of oneself…birds born in a cage think flying is an illness. It's hard to free fools from the chains they revere."

Toseima J- Coz, American actress.

275. "They say time is money, but really it's not. If we ever go broke, time is all we got."

J Cole, American rap artist.

276. "Those who can make you believe absurdities can make you commit atrocities."

Voltaire (1694-1778), French writer.

277. "I believe the major factor contributing to President Trump's popularity amongst the people, is, he's not a politician."

Irish political pundit.

278. "Definition of stupid; knowing the truth, seeing the truth, but still believing the lies."

279. "True love is when you love someone to your very last breath."

280. "I'm selfish, impatient, and a little insecure. I make mistakes, I am out of control at times, and hard to handle; but if you can't handle me at my worst, then you sure as hell don't deserve me at my best."

Marilyn Monroe (1926 -1962), American actress.

281. "I've heard of many tragic cases of walking, talking, normal children who wound up with profound mental disorders after vaccines."

Rand Paul, American Senator.

282. "Seldom do money and morality go hand in hand, for the energy that's attached to money, when you look around, has not been put to the greater good."

Author.

283. "All battles are fought by scared men who'd rather be someplace else."

John Wayne (1907-1979) American actor.

284. "I know you won't believe me, but the highest form of human excellence is to question oneself and others."

Socrates, philosopher.

285. "Driver carries no cash, he's married."

Sign displayed on the back of a commercial vehicle, Britain, 2011.

286. "If liberty means anything at all, it means the right to tell people what they don't want to hear."

George Orwell (1903-1950), novelist, writer, activist.

287. "Truth is what we hide; cover stories are what we sell."

Zerohedge.com, 2 June 2020.

288. "The Federal Reserve is a franchise of the Bank of England."

289. "When you control the media, you control public opinion."

290. "If you have no critics, you'll likely have no success."

Malcolm X (1925-1965), American minister/activist.

291. "For nothing is secret that shall not be made manifest; neither anything hid, that shall not be known and come abroad."

Luke 8:17, New American Standard Version, and a quote often found on The Q Pages.

292. "To one who has faith no explanation is necessary. To one without faith, no explanation is possible."

St. Thomas Aquinas (1225-1274), Italian Dominican friar, philosopher.

293. "If you are humble in victory, you will not be humiliated in defeat."

Author.

294. "A wise girl knows her limits; a smart girl knows that she has none."

Marilyn Monroe, American actress.

295. "You have to start with the truth. The truth is the only way we can get anywhere, because, any decision-making that is based upon lies or ignorance can't lead to a good conclusion."

Julian Assange, editor/activist.

296. "Desperation is the raw material of drastic change. Only those who can leave behind everything they have ever believed in, can hope to escape."

William S. Burroughs, American writer.

297. "In my great melancholy, I loved life – for I love my melancholy."

Soren Kierkegaard (1813-1855), Danish philosopher.

298. "We live in a world where we have to hide to make love, while violence is practiced in broad daylight."

John Lennon (1940-1980), singer/songwriter/activist.

299. "To find yourself, think for yourself."

Socrates, philosopher.

300. "We are born ignorant, but one must work hard to remain stupid."

Benjamin Franklin (1706-1790), Founding Father of the United States.

301. "Cooking is such a lovely way of showing how much you care for someone."

Ainsley Harriet, English chef.

302. "Only when the tide goes out, do you discover who's been swimming naked."

Warren Buffet, financier.

303. "There are only two things governments fear; the people coming together, and the truth."

Author.

304. "If we please you, tell others. If not, tell us."

Popular and widespread sign, noted by author in the Saucy Kipper chippie, London's East End.

305. "Is that truly you, master?"

Thomas, as he felt Jesus after the resurrection.

306. "There is nothing concealed that will not be disclosed or hidden that will not be made known."

Luke 12:2, New International Version.

307. "Sin has many tools, but a lie is the handle that fits them all."

Oliver Wendell Holmes (1809-1894), American physician.

308. "No one is useless in this world who lightens the burdens of another."

Charles Dickens (1812-1870), writer.

309. "Miracles start to happen when you give as much energy to your dreams as you do to your fears."

310. "What happens when you broadcast the truth, is, you piss everyone off."

Milton William Cooper (1943-2001), American author, American hero.

311. "Logic will get you from A to Z. Imagination will get you everywhere."

Albert Einstein (1879-1955), physicist.

312. "I try to live life so that I can live with myself."

John Green, American author.

313. "Muddy water is best cleared by leaving it alone."

Alan Watts (1915-1973), writer.

314. "It is better to change an opinion than persist in a wrong one."

Socrates, philosopher.

315. "He has a chance to be a hero, or Nero."

*Thomas Williams, 'Truth, Honour, and Integrity' show investigator/visionary activist
- referring to President Donald Trump, March 2020.*

316. "I have a condition that permits me from wearing a mask, it's called intelligence."

Poster, aim4truth.com, 10 July 2020.

317. "Don't just teach your children to read…teach them to question what they read; teach them to question everything."

George Carlin (1937-2008), American comedian.

318. "Don't think money does everything, or you are going to end up doing everything for money."

Voltaire (1694-1778), French writer.

319. "Vaccination is a barbarous practice and one of the most fatal of all delusions current in our time. Conscious objectors to vaccination should stand alone, if need be, against the whole world in defense of their conviction."

Mahatma Gandhi (1869-1948), Indian civil rights leader, activist, lawyer.

320. "The truth is I've never fooled anyone; I've let men sometimes fool themselves."

Marilyn Monroe (1926-1962), American actress.

321. "You can't fix it by continually electing the same politicians that broke it."

Author.

322. "It could almost have been designed by an architect, obviously it was."

Ray Mears, British woodsman and TV personality, referring to the Grass Tree on the TV series 'Wild Australia'.

323. "It is well the people of the nation do not understand our banking and monetary system, for, if they did, I believe there would be a revolution before tomorrow morning."

Henry Ford (1863-1947) American industrialist.

324. "I believe that banking institutions are more dangerous to our liberties than standing armies. If the American people ever allow private banks to control the issue of their currency, first by inflation, and then by deflation – the banks and corporations that will grow up around the banks will deprive people of their property, until their children wake up homeless on the continent their fathers conquered. The issuing power should be taken from the banks and restored to the people, to whom it properly belongs."

Thomas Jefferson (1801-1809), President of the United States.

325. "We create the rainbows; they are easy for us and still you are in wonder."

Sathya Sai Baba (1926-2011), Indian guru.

326. "Religion has actually convinced people that there's an invisible man living in the sky, who watches everything you do, of every minute of the day of your life. And, he has a list of ten things he does not want you to do, and if you do any of these ten things, he has a special place full of fire and smoke, and ash and tortures, where he will send you to suffer and burn, and scream and cry forever and ever, until the end of time…but he loves you anyway. He loves you, and he needs your money."

George Carlin (1937-2008), American comedian.

327. "Sometimes, I want to ask God why he allows poverty, famine and injustice in the world, when he could be doing something about it; but I'm afraid he might ask me the same question."

Charles Dickens (1812-1870), writer.

328. "Life is hard; it's harder if you're stupid."

John Wayne (1907-1979), American actor.

329. "To become who you truly are, you need to be honest with yourself."

330. "Love all, trust a few, do wrong to none."

'All's Well that End's Well, Act I, Scene I, William Shakespeare (1564-)1616 English poet/playwright.

331. "Sometimes, our dreams come true, sometimes our fears do too."

J. Cole, American rap artist.

332. "Skip the fluff, gets right to the stuff."

Marcus Allen, Running Back Los Angeles Raiders/Kansas City Chiefs.

333. "Often, when you think you are at the end of something, you're at the beginning of something else."

Fred Rogers (1928-2003), American TV personality.

334. "We know who you are, we saw what you did."

Punisher Q posts, March 2020, referring to the 'Deep State', a nefarious firm who run the world behind the façade of world governments.

335 "Violence is a disease, a disease that corrupts all who use it, regardless of the cause."

Chris Hedges, American journalist.

336. "Ultimately the definition of bravery is not being afraid of yourself."

Chogyam Trungpa Rinpoche (1939-1987), Teacher.

337. "There has never been a time when you and I have not existed, nor will there be a time when we cease to exist. As the same person inhabits the body through childhood, youth and old age, so too, at the time of death he attains another body. The wise are not deluded by these changes."

Krishna.

338. "I want to tell you something very clear: don't worry about American pressure on Israel. We, the Jewish people, control America, and the Americans know it."

Ariel Sharon (1928-2014), Israeli Prime Minister.

339. "Future proves past."

The Q Movement.

340. "Ridicule is man's most potent weapon."

Saul Alinsky (1909-1972), American activist.

341. "If you repeat a lie often enough, people will believe it, and you will even come to believe it yourself."

Joseph Goebbels (1887-1945), Reich Minister of Propaganda.

342. "When we hang the capitalists, they will sell us the rope."

Joseph Stalin (1878-1953), Premier of the Soviet Union.

343. "Any man who thinks he can be happy and prosperous by letting the government take care of him, better take a look at the American Indian."

Henry Ford, (1863-1947), American industrialist.

344. "The people get the government they deserve."

Linda Ridden, friend to the author and spiritualist.

345. "The truth is in the movies, and the lies are in the media."

346. "Turkeys don't vote for Christmas."

347. "It's not the government's job to protect my health. It's the government's job to protect my rights. It's my job to protect my health. When you trade liberty for safety, you end up loosening both."

348. "A business that makes nothing but money, is a poor business."

Henry Ford (1863-1947), American industrialist.

349. "One thing's for sure. If we keep doing what we're doing, we're going to keep getting what we're getting. One definition of insanity is to keep doing the same thing and expecting different results."

Stephen Covey (1932-2012) American educator.

350. "I am going to tell you like it is. I hope you can take it like it is."

Malcolm X (1925-1965) American minister/activist.

351. "There is never so great a good, as knowledge of the truth."

Aristotle, Greek philosopher.

352. "For there is never anything but the present, and if one cannot live there, one cannot live anywhere."

Alan Watts (1915-1973), writer.

353. "We must all face the facts that our leaders are certainly insane, or worse."

William S. Burroughs (1947-1997) American writer.

354. "Wherever there is a settled society, religion is necessary; the laws cover manifest crimes and religion covers secret crimes."

Voltaire (1694-1778), French writer.

355. "People who say it cannot be done, should not interrupt those who are doing it."

George B. Shaw (1856-1950), playwright.

356. "Self-worth is often tied to money, or, more commonly lack of money."

357. "Oh what a tangled web we weave, when first we practice to deceive."

Marmion, Sir Walter Scott, 1808.

358. "The conspiracy theory label was contrived by the CIA (Criminals In Action) to derail the truth movement."

359. "Everyone knew about the children getting in the back of Jimmy Savile's Rolls Royce; as long as they weren't their children, it was OK."

Janet Street Porter, journalist/presenter.

360. "A man is usually more careful of his money than he is of his principles.

Oliver Wendell Holmes, (1809-1894), American physician.

361. "Man will pay a heavy price in karma for his treatment of the animals."

White Eagle, spiritual teacher – channeled message.

362. "When they kept on questioning him, he straightened up and said to them 'Let he who is without sin be the first to throw a stone at her'. Again, he stooped down and wrote on the ground. At this, those who heard began to go away one at a time, the older ones first, until only Jesus was left, with the woman still standing there. Jesus straightened up and asked her 'Woman, where are they, has no-one condemned you?' 'No-one sir,' she said. 'Then neither do I condemn you,' Jesus declared. 'Go now and leave your life of sin.'"

John 8:7, New International Version

363. "If my dear friend Donald Trump ever decided to sacrifice his fabulous billionaire lifestyle to become President, he would become an unstoppable force for ultimate justice the Democrats and Republicans alike would celebrate."

George Magazine, June 1999, John F. Kennedy Jr (1960-1999), American lawyer.

364. "Talk's cheap."

Popular phrase, and a favourite of Lionel Reid, friend of the author.

365. "A government that withholds information in the interests of national security, or to protect state secrets, is essentially saying they realise that if the information became publicly available, it could provoke mass disturbance."

Author's note – codewords for protecting the corrupt elites.

366. "Why would the truth fear investigation? This is why political correctness was brought in, which in essence, is censorship."

367. "You can't fix stupid."

Ron White, American comedian.

368. "People demand freedom of speech as a compensation for the freedom of thought which they seldom use."

Soren Kierkegaard (1813-1855), Danish philosopher.

369. "Someday, you will be old enough to start reading fairy tales again."

C.S. Lewis (1898-1963), Irish writer.

370. "Knowledge is power, and power leads to resistance. Therefore, the way to eliminate resistance is cutting it off at source through censorship."

371. "Hell is empty, and all the devils are here."

The Tempest, Act I, Scene 2 - William Shakespeare (1554-1616), English playwright.

372. "Journalism is printing what someone else does not want printed. Everything else is public relations."

George Orwell (1903-1950), novelist/activist.

373. "There is only one corner of the universe you can be certain of improving, and that's to your own self."

Aldous Huxley (1894-1963), American writer.

374. "The most important thing in life is to stop saying 'I wish' and start saying 'I will'."

Charles Dickens, (1812-1870), writer.

375. "Tomorrow is the most important thing in your life. Comes into us at midnight very clean. It's perfect when it arrives, and it puts itself in our hands. It hopes we've learned something from yesterday."

John Wayne (1907-1979), American actor.

376. "The three most powerful addictions are heroin, carbohydrates, and a monthly salary."

Nassim Nicholas, Taleb essayist.

377. "We are leaving the Piscean age – which was a male energy governed by the mind, and entering the Aquarian age, which is a feminine energy governed from the heart. The me consciousness is over; this is now the 'we' consciousness."

Author.

378. "No-one rules if no-one obeys."

Tao Do - Japanese philosophy.

379. "To move the world, we must first move ourselves."

Socrates, philosopher.

380. "We've had a flu vaccine for 78 years; we still have the flu. Are you awake yet?"

Image taken from aim4truth.com, 1st August 2020.

381. "You can fool all the people some of the time, and some of the people all of the time; but you cannot fool all the people all the time."

Abraham Lincoln (1861-1865) President of the United States.

382. "Imagine if you will, a world where people believe that the temperature of the planet can be controlled by giving money to the government."

Q Drop 4077, 3 May 2020.

383. "Don't flatter yourself that friendship authorizes you to say disagreeable things to your intimates. The nearer you come into a relationship with a person, the more necessary do tact and courtesy become. Except in cases of necessity, which are rare, leave your friend to learn unpleasant things from his enemies; they are ready enough to tell them."

Oliver Wendell Holmes (1809-1894) American physician.

384. "They wouldn't give you the drippings from their nose."

Author's birth mother, Joyce McCartney (1828-1989), referring to elitist society.

385. "It is not a conspiracy, don't call it a conspiracy. It is all out in the open and it stands on the ignorance, apathy, and stupidity of the American people that is the foundation upon which the new world order is built."

William Milton Cooper (1943-2001), American author, American hero.

386. "In many ways, they are exactly the same as us."

Australian citizen, replying to a reporter's question regarding their thoughts on Princes William and Harry. How naïve and how far from the truth can you get? – Author's note.

387. "Just because it's all you want, doesn't mean it's all you need."

Kurt Cobain (1967-1994), American singer-songwriter.

388. "You never know how strong you are, till being strong is your only choice."

Bob Marley (1945-1981) Jamaican singer-songwriter.

389. "It is easier for a camel to go through the eye of a needle, than a rich man to enter into the kingdom of God."

Matthew 19:24, New American Standard Version.

390. "Walking with a friend in the dark is better than walking alone in the light."

Helen Keller (1880-1968) American author.

391. "London – that great cesspit into which all the loungers and idlers of the Empire are irresistibly drained."

Sir Arthur C. Doyle (1859-1930), writer.

392. "There are only two things we should fight for. One is the defense of our homes and the other is the bill of rights."

Major-General Smedley Butler (1881-1941), United States Marine.

393. "When it comes down to it, let them think what they want. If they care enough to bother with what I do, then I'm already better than them anyway."

Marilyn Monroe (1929-1962), American actress.

394. "Keep calm and abolish the monarchy."

395. "The whole problem with the world is that fools and fanatics are always so sure of themselves and wiser people are full of doubts."

George B. Shaw (1856-1950), playwright.

396. "I find television very educating; every time someone turns on the set, I go into another room and read a book."

Groucho Marx (1890-1997), American comedian.

397. "The greater our knowledge increases, the greater our ignorance unfolds."

John F. Kennedy (1917-1963), President of the United States.

398. "What's the difference between Mark Zuckerberg and me? I give private information on corporations to you for free, and I'm a villain. Zuckerberg gives your private information to corporations, and he's man of the year."

Julian Assange, editor/activist.

399. "And the organization is strong, and it has a lot of money, and the ties between the Israeli and American-Jewish establishment are very strong in this country."

Shulamit Aloni (1928-2014), former Israeli Minister of Education, founder of the Ratz Party.

400. "If you really think the environment is less important than the economy, try holding your breath while you count your money."

Dr. Guy McPherson, American scientist.

401. "I never worry about action, but only inaction."

Winston Churchill (1874-1965), British Prime-Minister.

402. "I have never let schooling interfere with my education."

Mark Twain (1835-1910), American writer.

403. "I fell in love the way you fall asleep, slowly, then all at once."

John Green, American author.

404. "Every light is not the sun."

Alexander the Great (356-323 BC), King of Macedon.

405. "To be able to think outside the box, one needs to understand what's in the box."

Author.

406. "There is no darkness but ignorance."

William Shakespeare (1554-1616), English poet/playwright.

407. "It is more important to know where you are going than to get there quickly. Do not mistake activity with achievement."

Socrates, philosopher.

408. "Never doubt that a small group of thoughtful, committed citizens can change the world, indeed it is the only thing that ever has."

Margarete Mead (1901-1978), American Cultural Anthropologist.

409. "They won't start the revolution without you."

Robinhoodrevival.com – Author's former blog.

410. "Family not only needs to consist of merely those who share blood, but also those whom we'd give blood."

Charles Dickens (1812-1870), English writer.

411. "Reality is created by the mind; we can change our reality by changing our mind."

Plato, philosopher.

412. "We are the ones we have been waiting for."

413. "It is a sign of human weakness when religion and sects and their false teachings are portrayed as instrument of what is creational, and the wisdom becomes unreal through this" Semajase (plejarem)

414. "You can't handle the truth!"

'A Few Good Men', Jack Nicholson, American actor.

415. "There is a huge pedophile ring operating in Hollywood, which includes the likes of Errol Flynn, Menachem Begin and various others, amounting to the great and the good."

Anthony Blunt (1907-1983), Queens Art Curator.

416. "Because we can't change what we are not willing to be responsible for owning."

The official site of Bashar, channeled by Darryl Anka, 21st July 2020.

417. "My grandmother wanted me to get a good education, so she kept me as far away from school as possible."

Margarete Mead, American Cultural Anthropologist.

418. "Profit is good, but greed is a dirty word."

Tina Huddleston, author's sister.

419. "There are no coincidences."

420. "There is wisdom of the head and wisdom of the heart."

Charles Dickens (1812-1870), writer.

421. "God does not play dice with the universe."

Albert Einstein (1879-1955), physicist.

422. "Just the facts, ma'am."

Joe Friday, Dragnet TV series.

423. "I've said repeatedly it's no longer going to be business as usual when the coronavirus is over, thank goodness."

Author.

424. "Aren't they the people you step over when leaving the opera?"

George Young, Baron Young of Cookham, ex-conservative government minister, when asked a question concerning the homeless.

425. "Inside me are two dogs. One is mean and evil, and the other is good – and they fight each other all the time. When asked which one wins, I answer 'the one I feed the most'."

Sitting Bull (1830-1895), Hunkpapa Lakota leader.

426. "Why me? Why not?"

427. "To touch the soul of another human being is to walk on holy ground."

Stephen Covey (1932-2012), American educator.

428. "It's only the land of the free and home of the brave till people start listening to what you have to say."

Lionel Reid, friend of author.

429. "Everything you've been told, turn on its head."

Sathya Sai Baba (1926-2011), Indian guru.

430. "If honesty were suddenly introduced into American life, the whole system would collapse."

George Carlin (1937-2008), American comedian.

431. "In reality, they're not after me, they're after you. I'm just in the way."

Donald J. Trump, President of the United States.

432. "From experience, I came to learn that ayahuasca bestows upon the user, knowledge about a variety of topics, not only consciousness and perception, but also leads one to realize that what we perceive is an illusion."

433. "You can't complete a puzzle with your face against the table, sometimes you have to step back and look at the big picture."

434. "When I was five-years-old, my mother always told me that happiness was the key to life. When I went to school, they asked me what I wanted to be when I grow up: I wrote down happy; they told me I didn't understand the assignment, and I told them they didn't understand life."

John Lennon (1940-1980), singer/songwriter/activist.

435. "I love everyone, I forgive everyone; I love myself; I forgive myself, thank you."

Mantra.

436. "God give me patience, quickly."

Geoffrey Cheeseman, friend and mentor of author.

437. "Democracy is two wolves and a lamb voting on what to have for lunch. Liberty is a well-armed lamb contesting the vote."

Benjamin Franklin (1706-1790), Founding Father of America.

438. "We can forgive a child who is afraid of the dark; the real tragedy of life is, when men are afraid of the light."

Plato, philosopher.

439. "Follow the white rabbit."

The Q Movement.

440. "Phone them and tell them I'm dead."

Molly Roberts, author's six-year-old niece, to her mother Elizabeth, when the school inquired as to why she was absent that day.

441. "Conspiracy theorists will soon be called historians; we are making history."

jamiehanna45, May 2020.

442. "If you fail to achieve your goal, change your strategy not your goal."

Lord Krishna.

443. "It is enough that people know there was an election. The people who cast the votes decide nothing. The people who count the votes decide everything."

Joseph Stalin (1878-1953), Premier of the Soviet Union.

444. "Harvard is a hedge fund with a university attached."

Zerohedge.com, April 21, 2020.

445. "Intelligence consists of ignoring things that are irrelevant."

Nassim Nicholas, Taleb essayist.

446. "Women are naturally more secretive, and they like to do their own secreting."

Sir Arthur Conan Doyle (1859-1930), writer.

447. "No one said it was going to be easy."

Geoffrey Cheeseman, author's friend and mentor.

448. "Take a chance and you may lose. Take not a chance, and you have already lost."

Soren Kierkegaard (1813-1885), Danish philosopher.

449. "There is no such thing as talent, only awareness."

Chogyam Trungpa Rinpoche (1939-1987), Teacher.

450. "Annual income £20, annual expenditure £19.19.6 – result happiness. Annual income £20, annual expenditure £20.0.6 – result misery."

'David Copperfield', Wilkins Micawber, Charles Dickens (1812-1870), English writer.

451. "Children must be taught how to think, not what to think."

Margarete Mead (1901-1978), American Cultural Anthropologist.

452. "There's going to be no more normal on this planet, as I have told you so many times before, and so it is."

Kryon channeled message, from the other side of life, March 31st, 2020.

453. "Democracy: I want nothing to do with a system which operates on a premise that my rights don't exist, simply because I am outnumbered."

R Lee Wrights (1958-2017), American politician.

454. "If it's all above board, why is it secret?"

Author.

455. "The way I see it, if you want the rainbow, you gotta put up with the rain."

Dolly Parton, American singer/actress.

456. "It's problem, reaction, solution – the modus operandi of the 'deep state'."

David Icke, journalist/writer/activist.

457. "I felt my whole personality transform when I put on the SS uniform, it was quite frightening."

Ralph Fiennes, actor, on playing Amon Goeth in Schindler's List.

458. "The man who dies thus rich, dies disgraced."

Andrew Carnegie (1835-1919), American industrialist.

459. "After a shooting spree, they always want to take the guns away from the people who didn't do it. I sure as hell wouldn't want to live in a society where the only people allowed guns are the police and the military."

William Burroughs (1914-1997), American writer.

460. "I'd rather be hated for who I am, than loved for who I am not."

Kurt Cobain (1967-1994), American singer-songwriter.

461. "I am a free spirit; some don't like that, but that's who I am."

Princess Dianna (1961-1997).

462. "Think about how stupid the average person is, and then realize that half of them are more stupid than that."

George Carlin (1937-2008), American comedian.

463. "Keep the Duke of Edinburgh's name out of it."

Lord Denning's brief regarding the Profumo Affair.

464. "Some people feel the rain; others just get wet."

Bob Marley (1945-1981), Jamaican singer-songwriter.

465. "Ascension is not about leaving the world; it's about bringing Heaven down to Earth."

466. "Unfettered capitalism is a revolutionary force that consumes greater and greater numbers of human lives, until it finally consumes itself."

Chris Hedges, American journalist.

467. "When you begin this journey, (the search for the truth), you'll soon discover it's stranger than Star Trek."

Geoffrey Cheeseman, author's friend and mentor.

468. "Too often, people think that solving the world's problems is based on conquering the Earth, rather than touching the earth, touching ground."

Chogyam Trungpa Rinpoche (1939-1987), Teacher.

469. "If wars can be started by lies, they can be stopped by the truth."

Julian Assange, editor/activist.

470. "By and large, language is a tool for concealing the truth."

George Carlin (1937-2008), American comedian.

471. "I told you I was ill."

Spike Milligan (1918-2002), Irish comedian, gravestone epitaph (in Latin).

472. "Courage is being afraid and going on the journey anyhow."

John Wayne (1907-1979), American actor.

473. "I have been bent and broken, but I hope into a better shape."

Charles Dickens (1812-1870), English writer.

474. "I don't want to make money; I just want to be wonderful."

Marilyn Monroe (1926-1962), American actress.

475. "No matter how great the talent or efforts, some things just take time. You cannot produce a baby in one month by getting nine women pregnant."

Warren Buffet, financier.

476. "Where we love is home, home that our feet may leave, but not our hearts."

Oliver Wendell Holmes (1809-1894), American physician.

477. "If they don't know your dreams, they can't shoot them down."

J. Cole, American rap artist.

478. "It is difficult to find happiness within oneself, but impossible to find it anywhere else."

Arthur Schopenhauer (1788-1860), philosopher.

479. "Under educated and over medicated."

Jaclyn Dunne, Holistic health practitioner.

480. "Is that a pistol in your pocket, or are you just happy to see me?"

Mae West (1893-1980), American actress.

481. "The Mafia is an illegal crime syndicate, that operates outside of the law. Here in Britain, we've gone one better; the 'Mafia' has been empowered into the state. People know them as Lords, Sirs, Barons, Ladies, Princes, Princesses, Dukes, Duchesses, Baronesses, Marquis, Marchionesses, Earls, Viscounts, and Viscountesses; they have served the State with honor, to the detriment of the people. The list of honors is long, for we have many criminals operating here."

Author.

482. "Knowledge is power, and power is resistance; therefore, the way to eliminate resistance is cutting it off at source – censorship."

483. "We have an army of digital soldiers."

General Michael Thomas Flynn, former National Security Advisor to the Trump White House.

484. "Money and misery."

Author's birth mother, Joyce McCartney (1828-1989), noting how people who have wealth often seem to lack happiness.

485. "We have produced a study indicating, that if there were no secrets, the world economy could grow six-fold."

Massachusetts Institute of Technology.

486. "Time is very short for those who wait; very fast for those who are scared. Very long for those who lament; very short for those who celebrate. But, for those who love, time is eternal."

William Shakespeare (1554-1616) English poet/playwright.

487. "Free at last, free at last, thank God Almighty, we are free at last."

Martin Luther King Jr (1929-1968), American minister/activist.

488. "Bad business, is worse than no business."

Peter McCartney (1954-2016), Author's brother.

489. "We now live in a nation where doctors destroy health, lawyers destroy justice, universities destroy knowledge, the governments destroy freedom, the press destroys information, religion destroys morals, and our banks destroy the economy."

Chris Hedges, American journalist.

490. "Truth is learned, not taught."

The Q Movement.

491. "If John Brennan doesn't have a lawyer now, he'd better get one, because the indictments ae coming."

Joe di Genova, American lawyer, 13th April 2020

492. "The illegal we do immediately; the unconstitutional takes a little longer."

Henry Kissinger, former Secretary of State, USA.

493. "Look, the average Democrat voter is just plain stupid!"

Hillary Rodham Clinton, former Secretary of State, USA.

494. "The coronavirus will end when enough people have had enough."

Author, May 2020.

495. "The more we do to you, the less you seem to believe we are doing it."

Josef Mengele (1911-1979), German SS Officer and physician, AKA 'The Angel of Death'.

496. "I don't know what will happen now; we've got some difficult days ahead. But it really doesn't matter to me now, because I've been to the mountaintop. And I don't mind. Like anybody, I would like to live a long life – longevity has its place. But I'm not concerned about that now. I just want to do God's will. And he's allowed me to go up to the mountain. And I've looked over, and I've seen the Promised Land. I may not get there with you. But I want you to know, tonight, that we as a people, will get to the Promised Land. And so, I'm happy tonight; I'm not worried about anything; I'm not fearing any man. My eyes have seen the glory of the coming of the Lord."

Martin Luther King Jr (1929-1968), American minister/activist. (Author's note – this is my favourite quote).

497. "A psychotic is a guy who's just found out what's going on."

William S. Burroughs (1914-1997), American writer.

498. "Spirituality is being in touch within and of yourself."

499. "I am trying to find myself, sometimes that's not easy."

Marilyn Monroe (1926-1962), American actress.

500. "Beware of useful idiots. 'How to create a social state'. There are eight levels of control that must be obtained before you are able to create a social state. The first is the most important 1. Healthcare 2. Poverty 3. Debt 4. Gun control 5. Welfare 6. Education 7. Religion 8. Class warfare; are you just their useful idiot?"

Saul Alinsky (1909-1972), American activist.

501. "Today's truth is often the strange source of tomorrow's science fiction."

502. "It's not only what you don't know that hurts you; it's what you think you know, and don't, that get you."

503. "It is easier to perceive error than find truth, for the former lies on the surface, and is easily seen, while the latter lies in the depths, where few are willing to search for it."

Johann Wolfgang Von Goethe (1749-1832), writer.

504. "It is the first responsibility of every citizen to question authority."

Benjamin Franklin (1706-1790) Founding Father of the United States.

505. "The intuitive mind is a sacred gift and the rational mind is a faithful servant. We have created a society that honors the servant and has forgotten the gift."

Albert Einstein (1879-1955), physicist.

506. "Your mind will answer most questions if you learn to relax and wait for the answer."

William S. Burroughs (1914-1997), American writer.

507. "Military men are dumb, stupid animals, to be used as pawns in foreign policy."

Henry Kissinger, former Secretary of State, USA.

508. "Sometimes, you put up walls not to keep people out, but to see who cares enough to break them down."

Socrates, philosopher.

509. "The realest people don't have a lot of friends."

Tupac Shakur (1971-1996), American rap artist.

510. "A word to the one percent. You control our world. You've poisoned the air we breathe, contaminated the water we drink, and copyrighted the food we eat. We fight in your wars, die for your causes, and sacrifice our freedoms to protect you. You've liquidated our savings, destroyed our Middle Class, and used our tax dollars to bail out your unending greed. We are slaves to your corporations, zombies to your airwaves, servants to your decadence. You've stolen our elections, assassinated our leaders, and abolished our rights as human beings. You own our property, shipped away our jobs, and shredded our unions. You've profited off disaster, destabilized our currencies, and raised our cost of living. You've monopolized our freedom, stripped away our education, and almost extinguished our flame. We are hit…we are bleeding…but we ain't got time to bleed. We will bring the giants to their knees, and you will witness our revolution!"

Jessie Ventura, American politician/activist.

511. "When man to man shall be friend and brother."

Gerald Massey (1828-1907), English poet.

512. "Every man is guilty of all the good he didn't do."

Voltaire (1694-1778), French writer.

513. "If you're not careful, the newspapers will have you hating the people who are being oppressed and loving the people who are doing the oppressing."

Malcolm X (1925-1965), American minister/activist.

514. "A man is known by the silence he keeps."

Oliver Herford (1863-1935), writer.

515. "Woe unto him that call evil good and good evil that put darkness for light and light for darkness; that put bitter for sweet and sweet for bitter."

Isaiah 5:20, New American Standard Version.

516. "Never attribute to malice that which can be adequately explained by stupidity."

517. "After one look at the planet, any visitor from outer space would say 'I want to see the manager'."

William S. Burroughs (1914-1997), American writer.

518. "It is difficult to free fools from the chains they revere."

Voltaire (1694-1778), French writer.

519. "When I was a boy and I would see scary things in the news, my mother would say to me 'look for the helpers. You will always find people who are helping'. To this day, especially in times of disaster, I remember my mother's words and I am always comforted by realizing that there are so many helpers, so many caring people in the world."

Fred Rogers (1928-2003), American TV presenter.

520. "What, then, shall we say in response to these things? If God is for us, who can be against us?"

Romans 8:31, New International Version.

521. "Nothing lasts forever, but at least we get these memories."

J. Cole, American rap artist.

522. "If you think you can do a thing, or think you can't do a thing, you're right."

Henry Ford (1863-1947) American industrialist.

523. "Mr. McCartney, avoid aluminium like the plague."

Dr. Davis, author's doctor/holistic practitioner, in the 80s. (Aluminium products were classed as carcinogenic many years later).

524. "A scholar tries to learn something every day; a student of Buddhism ties to unlearn something daily."

Alan Watts (1915-1973), writer.

525. "Beware of false knowledge; it is more dangerous than ignorance."

George B. Shaw (1856-1950), playwright.

526. "There is no use whatsoever trying to help people who do not help themselves."

Andrew Carnegie (1835-1919), American industrialist.

527. "Everything's easy; humans make it difficult."

Danny Searle, YouTube, spiritual teacher.

528. "Always remember that you are absolutely unique, just like everyone else."

Margarete Mead (1901-1978), American cultural anthropologist.

529. "The key is not to prioritize what's on your schedule, but to schedule your priorities."

Stephen Covey (1932-2012), American educator.

530. "Peaceful noncompliance will bring the global control system to its knees."

robinhoodrevival.com.

531. "We will drain the swamp in Washington D.C. and replace it with a new government of, and by, and for the people."

Donald J. Trump, President of the United States.

532. "Imagine a virus so deadly that media and government have to fabricate death numbers to make people believe it's real."

Message on a poster, America, August 2020.

533. "A government that robs Peter to pay Paul, can always depend on the support of Paul."

George B. Shaw (1856-1950), playwright.

534. "I swore never to be silent whenever, or wherever, human beings endure suffering and humiliation. We must always take sides. Neutrality helps the oppressor, never the victim. Silence encourages the tormentor, never the tormented."

Elie Wiesel (1928-2019), American-Romanian writer.

535. "The comfort of the rich depends upon an abundant supply of the poor."

Voltaire (1694-1778), French writer.

536. "They must find it difficult – those who have taken authority as truth, rather than truth as authority."

Gerald Massey (1828-1907), English poet.

537. "Political language is designed to make lies sound truthful, and murder respectable."

George Orwell (1903-1950), novelist/visionary.

538. Don't find fault, find a remedy; anybody can complain."

Henry Ford (1863-1947), American industrialist.

539. "If a man empties his purse into his head, no man can take it away from him. An investment in knowledge always pays the best interest."

Benjamin Franklin (1706-1790), Founding Father of the United States.

540. "Convenience is the most common growth of the control system."

Thomas Williams, 'Truth, Honour, and Integrity' show investigator/visionary activist.

541. "You only live once; but if you do it right, once is enough."

Mae West (1893-1990), American actress.

542. "The rich rule America because of a system wherein money translates directly into political power."

Zerohedge.com, 3/19/2018.

543. "It's easier to fool people than convince them they have been fooled."

Mark Twain (1835-1910), American writer.

544. "If you really want to help your children, leave them alone."

George Carlin (1937-2008), American comedian.

545. "War is a racket. It always has been. It is possibly the oldest, surely the most vicious. It is conducted for the benefit of the very few, at the expense of the very many."

Major-General Smedley Butler (1881-1940), US Army.

546. "Black lives matter. All lives matter; race is another divide and conquer program to keep the folks in line, from coming together and taking on the real issues."

Author.

547. "Evil indeed is the man who has not one woman to mourn him."

Sir Arthur Conan Doyle (1859-1930), author.

548. "True friends are like stars; you can only recognize them when it's dark around you."

Bob Marley (1945-1981), Jamaican singer-songwriter.

549. "To achieve goals you've never achieved before; you need to start doing things you've never done before."

Steve Covey (1932-2012), American educator.

550. "You are an aperture through which the universe is looking at and exploring itself."

Alan Watts (1915-1973), writer.

551. "Freeing the MSM from the shackles of plutocracy, necessarily means combating the mind-viruses being dumped into their heads, by toxic establishment war machines like the Washington Post."

Zerohedge.com, 1/9/2017.

552. "When you stop growing, you start dying."

William S. Burroughs (1914-1997), American writer.

553. "Not knowing the truth doesn't make you ignorant; not wanting to know the truth is what makes you ignorant."

Anonymous.

554. "He's the best boy in the girl's class."

Alfred McCartney (1917-1990), author's father, referring to his younger brother's behaviour in school.

555. "Falling down is not a failure. Failure comes when you stay where you have fallen."

Socrates, philosopher.

556. "When you show deep empathy towards others, their defensive energy goes down and positive energy replaces it. That's when you can get more creative in solving problems."

Steve Covey, American educator.

557. "To make the rich work harder, you pay them more; to make the poor work harder, you pay them less."

558. "What people say, what people do, and what they say they do are entirely different things."

Margarete Mead (1901-1978), American cultural anthropologist.

559. "Coming together is a beginning, staying together is progress, and working together is success."

Henry Ford (1863-1947), American industrialist.

560. "Foreign aid is given by poor people in rich countries; to the rich in poor countries."

561. "Sadly, this nation, Britain, will be the last to emerge from the darkness."

David Icke, journalist/writer/activist, referring to the United Kingdom.

562. "If the Catholic Church were to sell the land they own in Brazil alone, there would be plenty of money from the sale to end world poverty."

563. "Google, in reality, is Skynet."

Robinhoodrevival.com – author's former blog.

564. "Nanny, is this the worst birthday present you've ever had?"

Rocky Frost, author's five-year-old grandson, commenting on the (awful) meal his daughter and son-in-law paid for, at Dana Point, California, for his wife's birthday.

565. "It is far better to keep the British as your enemy. With an enemy, you are constantly on your guard; having them as a friend relaxes your attention, as their duplicity knows no boundaries."

Arabian political commentator.

566. "I wish they'd taught me the laws of karma at school. It would certainly have made my life a whole lot easier."

Author.

567. "My treasure lies in my friends."

Alexander the Great (365-323 BC), King of Macedon and Ancient Greece.

568. "While I'm dying in the loneliness of the covid lockdown isolation, I came here to listen to this life-long masterpiece...'Now I've said too much...I'm just losing my depression. Thanks R.E.M."

Comment on YouTube 'Losing My Religion', official video, 15th April 2020.

569. "Never forget the devil is very cunning; but remember that God is very clever."

Hazel Abel, author's friend and mentor.

570. "I have lost count the number of times she has rescued my humanity."

Author, referring to his wife.

571. "We live in a debt based, harvesting system."

Thomas Williams, 'Truth, Honour, and Integrity' show investigator/visionary activist.

572. "God, please give me the grace to accept the things I cannot change; and grant unto me the power to change the things I cannot accept."

573. "I prefer insurrection over tyranny."

French Resistance Worker.

574. "The people who are trying to make this world worse are not taking the day off; why should I?"

Bob Marley (1945-1981), Jamaican singer-songwriter.

575. "Mike, you could write a book on what you know and fill a library with what you don't."

Heather Cheeseman, author's friend and mentor.

576. "Angels of power, angels of light, flood my soul with Christ consciousness".

Daily mantra, to be said three times – from Beulah Hudson, author's friend and spiritualist.

577. "My dear man, you were not brought into this world to rely on anyone."

Dr. Davis, 1984 – author's doctor, holistic practitioner.

578. *Author's note. Check out the YouTube video of Tina Turner performing the peace mantra 'Sarvesham Svastir Bhavatu'. It is immensely powerful, and I believe holds huge importance to our future.*

579. "In the age of information, knowledge is a choice."

580. "You have to be in it to win it."

581. "There's Agent Smiths everywhere, Dad."

Dan McCartney, our sone referring to the movie 'The Matrix', and the vast majority of the British people's reaction to the coronavirus, especially.

582. "Do not go gently into that goodnight, but rage, rage against the dying of the light."

Dylan Thomas (1914-1953), Welsh poet.

583. "A plumber installs two to three fail safes in a central heating system to prevent it from overheating. The human body has 3,500."

584. "If it's not broken, don't fix it."

585. "See, the difference between Britain and America is when I drive my Rolls Royce in LA, people look at me and say wow, how can I get myself into one of those cars? In Britain, they say, how can we get him out of that car?"

Michael Caine, English actor.

586. "I would rather be uncomfortable with the truth, than be lied to in comfort. That's just my nature."

Jessie Ventura, American politician, actor, professional wrestler.

587. "When will man be ready to go to God? Sadly, not until he's on his knees."

Sathya Sai Baba (1926-2011), Indian guru.

588. "Well put it this way, if there were no bars on the windows, I would have thrown myself out."

Donald. J. Trump, President of the United States, replying to reporter regarding the first security briefing after his inauguration.

589. "God is the only one, his name is true. He is the creator. He is without fear. He is inimitable to none. He never dies. He is beyond births and deaths. He is self-illuminated. He is realized by the kindness of the true guru. Repeat his name. He was true in the beginning; he was true when the ages commenced, and he is also true now."

Sikh prayer.

590. "Foreign aid is a gigantic slush fund, used by unscrupulous politicians and bankers to feather their own nests and finance black (off the book) projects."

Author.

591. "The heart chakra is mission control."

592. "Educate and inform the whole mass of people. They are the only sure reliance for the preservation of our liberty."

Thomas Jefferson (1743-1826), American statesman, founding father, and 3rd President of the United States.

593. "There's no honor, it's all gone. Time was, the guilty party and would be summoned to the chairman's office. Knocking on his door, they would be told to enter and sit down at his desk. On the desk would be a glass a decanter of brandy, and a gun. The chairman would pour a glass and leave this office. After the shot was fired, the coup de grace – the body would be taken away and the mess cleaned up. Today, when summoned to the chairman's office, the guilty party walks in not bothering to knock, puts their feet on the desk and pours themselves a stiff one. As the chairman leaves the room, they shoot him in the back and proceed to finish the decanter."

Political observation, Britain in the 1970s.

594. "They got money for the war but can't feed the poor."

Tupac Shakur (1971-1996), American rap artist.

595. "The truth will always win."

WikiLeaks.

596. "The media is the enemy of the people."

597. "Educate before you vaccinate."

598. "A problem shared is a problem halved."

599. "Never give negativity an inch; before you know it, it would have consumed a mile."

Author.

600. "The world has enough for everyone's needs; but not everyone's greed."

Mahatma Gandhi (1869-1948), Indian activist/leader/lawyer.

601. "When the state puts you in jail for walking in a park with your child because it's too dangerous, but let's criminals out of jail, then it's not about your health."

Kevin Sorbo, American actor, referring to Democratic State Governor's during Covid 19.

602. "American retail has shifted overnight from what people want, to what people need."

Analyst, April 2020.

603. Rules for Radicals. "Create crises – make the people believe that a crisis exists and that the only solution is more government programs. It is not important whether or not a crisis actually exists, it is only important that people believe it to be so" Saul Alinsky 1909 – 1972 American Activist.

604. "They get the shot, that night they have a fever of 103, they go to sleep...and three months later, their brain is gone."

Robert F. Kennedy Jnr, American attorney.

605. "Doctors spend seven years in university studying to be a doctor, they don't spend one hour on healing you. Once qualified as a doctor, they are called practitioners. They then proceed to practice on you."

Thomas Williams, 'Truth, Honour, and Integrity' show investigator/visionary activist.

606. "What goes around, comes around. The almighty may be slow, but he's sure."

Author's mother.

607. "In the temple of my mind, no space exists for negative energies, negative thought, negative feelings."

Mantra, given and used by Linda Ridden, author's friend/mentor.

608. "There are lies, damned lies, and statistics."

Mark Twain (1835-1919), American writer.

609. "Yesterday is history, tomorrow is a mystery; today is a gift, that's why it's called the present."

K. P. Kelly, administrator 'thefederationoflight.ning', Monday 27 April, 2020.

610. "The truth is guarded by the divine."

611. "Sadly in this age, it's what you've got that important, not who you are."

Author.

612. "Everyone you meet always asks you if you have a career, are you married, or own a house – as if life was some kind of grocery list. But no-one ever asks you if you are happy."

Heath Ledger, (1979-2008), Australian actor.

613. "If that f**king bastard wins, we all hang from nooses."

Hilary Clinton, former First Lady and Secretary of State, USA – email to Donna Brazile, 17th October 2016, regarding Donald J. Trump becoming president.

614. "Follow the money, and you will know who to prosecute."

Starshipearththebogpicture.com

615. "I resolved to stop accumulating and begin the infinitely more serious and difficult task of wise distribution."

Andrew Carnegie (1835-1919), American industrialist.

616. "The deep state whispered to President Trump 'you cannot withstand the storm'. The President whispered back 'I am the storm.'"

Taken from a poster during Donald J. Trump's first term as President of the United States.

617. "He's more trouble than a wagon load of monkeys."

Author's birth mother, Joyce McCartney (1828-1989), referring to his younger brother, Clive McCartney.

618. "One must never turn their back on evil, this is a lesson we have all paid heavily for."

Thomas Williams, 'Truth, Honour, and Integrity' show investigator/visionary activist.

619. "From a time when medicine actually was about curing people and not treating them, words f**king matter. That's what the left despises."

Tweet, The First Circle (Dante's Inferno), 26th April 2020, referring to a copy of a medical magazine dated 1899.

620. "There is no greater tyranny than that which is perpetrated under the shield of law and in the names of justice."

Charles de Montesquieu (1689-1755), French philosopher.

621. "Learn to value yourself, which means fight for your happiness."

Ayn Rand (1905-1982), writer.

622. "You will not serve yourself by being the richest man in the cemetery."

623. "Once the truth comes out, the whole truth, and nothing but the truth, the British people will raise to the ground the palaces of Westminster, Kensington and Buckingham, the Bank of England, New Scotland Yard, the Ministry of Defense, and the Department for Health and Social Security, topped off with funeral pyres, for starters. For we want no traces left, no monuments, no graven images to evil in our new world of love, light and truth."

Author.

624. "No disease, including cancer, can exist in an alkaline environment."

Dr. Otto Warburg (1883-1970), Nobel prize winner for cancer discovery.

625. "Enter into his gates with thanksgivings, and into his courts with praise: be thankful unto him and bless his name. For the Lord is good; his mercy is everlasting; and his truth endureth to all generations."

Psalm 100, 4-5, New International Version.

626. "If you wish to know what happened to Michael, follow the money trail."

La Toya Jackson, American singer, when questioned concerning the death of her brother.

627. "Half the truth is often a great lie."

Benjamin Franklin (1706-1790) Founding Father of the United States.

628. "The light of the righteous shines brightly, but the lamp of the wicked is extinguished."

Proverbs 13, New International Version.

629. "People fall into a trap that CNN has to report it to be true."

Paladin, The White Hats Report, A Kerry Cassidy interview, YouTube.

630. "All is not what it seems."

Popular phrase and a favourite of the author.

631. "Marriage is a great institution, but I'm not ready for an institution."

Mae West (1893-1980), American actress.

632. "The masks on, walks outside and while driving your car is mind blowing to me. Do you not know how unhealthy it is to keep inhaling your carbon dioxide and restricting proper oxygen flow? I honestly cannot believe how non-logical we have become! We, as a society, seem to just listen to (perceived) authority without question. I don't see a whole lot of critical thought happening here, I'm sorry to say. Why I opt not to wear a mask, well, let me break it down for you; the body requires ample amounts of oxygen for optimal immune health, especially during a so-called 'pandemic'. Proper oxygenation of your cells and blood is essential for the body to function as it needs, in order to fight off any illness."

Dr. Judy Mikovits, former American research scientist.

633. "My people are destroyed from lack of knowledge."

Hosea 4:6, New International Version.

634. "There's a spike in coronavirus because there's a spike in testing...if we gave more IQ tests, there would be a spike in morons."

Poster, aim4truth.com, 9th July 2020.

635. "The finest antidote against vaccines ever created is a mother's breast milk."

Author.

636. "The media is the devil's mouthpiece."

starshipearththebigpicture.com, 6 June 2020.

637. "Truth is, the Federal Reserve is not federal, and it's got no reserve."

638. "The difference between genius and stupidity, is that genius has its limits."

Albert Einstein (1879-1955), physicist.

639. "The basic principle of state capitalism is that cost and risk and socialized, while profit is privatized."

Noam Chomsky, American philosopher/activist.

640. "There are no limits to the amount of good you can do if you don't care who gets the credit."

Ronald Reagan, (1911-2004), Actor/President of the United States, 1981-89.

641. "Compassion automatically invites you to relate to people, because you no longer regard people as a drain on your energy."

Chogyam Trungpa Rinpoche (1939-1987), teacher.

642. "Without free speech, no search for truth is possible; without free speech, no discovery of truth is useful."

Charles Bradlaugh (1833-1891), English political activist.

643. "I love you, I am sorry, please forgive me, thank you."

Morrah Nalamaku Simeona (1913-1992), Ho'oponopono prayer

644. "Do right, risk the consequences."

Bon Enyart, Pastor.

645. "There is nothing more deceptive than an obvious fact."

Sir Arthur Conan Doyle (1859-1930), writer.

646. "Those who arrested Anne Frank and saw to her murder were obeying the law. Those who shielded her and kept her safe, were breaking the law."

647. "It's not the men in your life that matters; it's the life in your men."

Mae West (1893-1980), American actress.

648. "If you can make it through the night there's a brighter day" Tupac Shakur 1971 – 1996 American Wrapper.

649. "Hell have no fury like a woman scorned."

William Congreve (1670-1729), Playwright.

650. "There is peace even in storm."

Vincent van Gogh (1853-1890), Dutch artist.

651. "If you feel like you don't fit into this world, it is because you are here to help build another one."

652. "This little light of mine I'm goin' to let it shine."

653. "Whenever you find yourself on the side of the majority, it's time to pause and reflect."

Mark Twain (1835-1910), American writer.

654. "We'll know our disinformation program is complete when everything the American public believes is false."

William Casey (1913-1987), CIA Director 1981-1987. "Criminals in Action" – author's note.

655. "It's only your mind that holds you back."

Sathya Sai Baba (1926-2011), Indian guru.

656. "I can't believe how easy it is to come and visit you."

Alfred Bird (1929-1999), author's father-in-law, to his daughter in a dream, referring to the ease of moving between dimensions.

657. "I'm sorry, but I don't want to be an emperor. That's not my business. I don't want to rule or conquer anyone. I should like to help everyone - if possible - Jew, Gentile - black man - white. We all want to help one another. Human beings are like that. We want to live by each other's happiness - not by each other's misery. We don't want to hate and despise one another. In this world there is room for everyone. And the good earth is rich and can provide for everyone. The way of life can be free and beautiful, but we have lost the way.

Greed has poisoned men's souls, has barricaded the world with hate, has goose-stepped us into misery and bloodshed. We have developed speed, but we have shut ourselves in. Machinery that gives abundance has left us in want. Our knowledge has made us cynical. Our cleverness, hard and unkind. We think too much and feel too little. More than machinery we need humanity. More than cleverness we need kindness and gentleness. Without these qualities, life will be violent and all will be lost....

The aeroplane and the radio have brought us closer together. The very nature of these inventions cries out for the goodness in men - cries out for universal brotherhood - for the unity of us all. Even now my voice is reaching millions throughout the world - millions of despairing men, women, and little children - victims of a system that makes men torture and imprison innocent people.

To those who can hear me, I say - do not despair. The misery that is now upon us is but the passing of greed - the bitterness of men who fear the way of human progress. The hate of men will pass, and dictators die, and the power they took from the people will return to the people. And so long as men die, liberty will never perish. ....

Soldiers! don't give yourselves to brutes - men who despise you - enslave you - who regiment your lives - tell you what to do - what to think and what to feel! Who drill you - diet you - treat you like cattle, use you as cannon fodder. Don't give yourselves to these unnatural men - machine men with machine minds and machine hearts! You are not machines! You are not cattle! You are men! You have the love of humanity in your hearts! You don't hate! Only the unloved hate - the unloved and the unnatural! Soldiers! Don't fight for slavery! Fight for liberty!

In the 17th Chapter of St Luke it is written: "the Kingdom of God is within man" - not one man nor a group of men, but in all men! In you! You, the people have the power - the power to create machines. The power to create happiness! You, the people, have the power to make this life free and beautiful, to make this life a wonderful adventure.

Then - in the name of democracy - let us use that power - let us all unite. Let us fight for a new world - a decent world that will give men a chance to work - that will give youth a future and old age a security. By the promise of these things, brutes have risen to power. But they lie! They do not fulfil that promise. They never will!

Dictators free themselves but they enslave the people! Now let us fight to fulfil that promise! Let us fight to free the world - to do away with national barriers - to do away with greed, with hate and intolerance. Let us fight for a world of reason, a world where science and progress will lead to all men's happiness. Soldiers! in the name of democracy, let us all unite!

Final speech from the movie 'The Great Dictator', 1940. Author's note – a message for all humanity as relevant today as the day it was first broadcast.

658. "The ones you love are usually the ones you take it out on."

659. "The illusion of freedom will continue as long as it's profitable to continue the illusion. At the point where the illusion becomes too expensive to maintain, they will take down the scenery, move the tables and chairs out of the way, then they will pull back the curtains and you will see the brick wall at the back of the theatre."

Frank Zappa (1940-1993), American instrumentalist.

660. "A single person who stops lying can bring down a tyranny."

Alexandra Solzhenitsyn (1918-2008), Russian novelist.

661. "Throw away your smartphone and take your life back."

662. "When we look in the mirror and we've done the work we're okay with, what is being reflected back to us?"

Jenny Constantine, Project 45:5D.

663. "Just remember that sometimes, the way you think about a person, isn't the way they actually are."

John Green, American author.

664. "If democrats are willing to cause such destruction in the pursuit of power, just imagine what they'll do if they obtain it."

Donald J. Trump, President of the United States.

665. "They lied about thalidomide. They lied about tobacco. They lied about asbestos. They lied about mercury. They lied about opioids. They're lying about vaccines. They lied about alluminium in deodorants. They lied about talc hygiene products. They lied about hormone replacement therapy. They lied about lead in paint. They lied about fluoride. They lied about antibiotics. They lied about saturated fats. They lied about raw milk. They lied about pesticides. They lied about GMOs. They lied about natural medicine. They lied about climate change. They lied about soy. They lied about artificial sweeteners. They lied about LED light bulbs. They lie about mercury fillings. They lied about RF radiation. They lied about glyphosate. They're lying about FluMist. They're lying about statins. They lied about sugar. They lied about processed food. They're lying about chemotherapy and radiotherapy. They lied about steroids. But they're telling you the truth about COVID-19?"

666. "The Amish community were asked why the coronavirus was not affecting them. They said 'we do not have television'.

Comments section, Anna Brees, YouTube, October 2020

667. "The news is sometimes created, but always curated. The latter is more pernicious. On any given day, there are thousands of potential stories. By picking which stories are written about and how prominently they're placed, a handful of publishers control much of the public narrative.

Elon Musk, Innovator and Entrepreneur.

668. "Once we rid ourselves of secrets, we discover euphoric peace. All evil and demonic intentions are created under a veil of secrecy."

Tweet, @TheBodNoMercy, 4ᵗʰ September 2020.

669. "When the debate is lost, slander becomes the tool of losers."

Socrates, philosopher.

670. "How can you tell the truth is being told? When Facebook blocks it; Twitter deletes it; Google hides it; YouTube bans it; Your government forbids it, and the media brands it a conspiracy theory".

Tweet, Jon Kirby, @jonkirbysthlm, 7th September 2020.

671. "Trust me, I know what I'm doing"

The Universe.

Printed in Great Britain
by Amazon

48356796R00063